BRUCE & STAN'S®

POCKET GUIDE TO

# ISLAM

BRUCE BICKEL and STAN JANTZ

D0064135

**HARVEST HOUSE PUBLISHERS**
Eugene, Oregon 97402

*Cover by Left Coast Design, Portland, Oregon*

*Cover illustration by Krieg Barrie Illustrations, Hoquiam, Washington*

## BRUCE & STAN'S® POCKET GUIDE TO ISLAM

Copyright © 2002 by Bruce Bickel and Stan Jantz
Published by Harvest House Publishers
Eugene, Oregon 97402

Library of Congress Cataloging-in-Publication Data
Bickel, Bruce, 1952–
   Bruce & Stan's pocket guide to Islam / Bruce Bickel and Stan Jantz.
      p. cm.
   ISBN 0-7369-1009-3 (pbk.)
   1. Islam—Controversial literature. 2. Islam—Relations—Christianity.
   3. Christianity and other religions—Islam.   I. Title: Bruce and Stan's
   pocket guide to Islam.   II. Title: Pocket guide to Islam.   III. Title:
   Guide to Islam.   IV. Jantz, Stan, 1952–   V. Title.
   BT1170 .B54 2002
   261.2'7—dc21                      2001006974

**Printed in the United States of America**

02  03  04  05  06  07  08  09  10 / BP-CF/ 10  9  8  7  6  5  4  3  2  1

# Contents

A Note from the Authors . . . . . . . . . . . . . .  5

1. Finding Your Religion: What You
   Believe Really Matters . . . . . . . . . . . . . . . .  13

2. All About Allah: Is "God" by
   Another Name the Same? . . . . . . . . . . . . .  29.

3. Holy Book Comparison: Are the Bible
   and the Qur'an Equally Reliable?  . . . . . .  45

4. Who Are Those Guys?: The Significance
   of Muhammad and Jesus  . . . . . . . . . . . . .  65

5. Sin and Salvation: You Can't Have
   One Without the Other  . . . . . . . . . . . . . . .  83

6. Death & Beyond: Judgment &
   Eternity in the Afterlife  . . . . . . . . . . . . . .  101

7. Sharing Your Faith: God's Good
   News Is for Everyone  . . . . . . . . . . . . . . . .  117

About the Authors  . . . . . . . . . . . . . . . . . . .  128

# A Note from the Authors

If you have read any of our other books—we've written more than 30 of them—then you know that we are very interested in God. Although we don't take ourselves too seriously, we are very serious about our faith. We think it matters. For this reason, we have always had more than a slight interest in other religions, but we have never considered it our responsibility to argue and debate with someone of another faith and exhaust them to a point of conversion. We are not into brow-beating, finger-wagging, or even Bible-thumping. We have always thought that it is enough to be able to explain, calmly and rationally, the basis for our faith in salvation through Jesus Christ. We even wrote a book about it: *Bruce & Stan's® Pocket Guide to Sharing Your Faith*.

Sharing what you believe requires that you know what you believe. Duh. That's why our books always emphasize the basic concepts of Christianity. That has been our focus. Until recently, we never got bogged down with the concepts of other beliefs and

religions because we were concentrating on what the Bible says about God, Jesus, and being a Christian. We figured that we would handle the viewpoints of other religions only as we got into discussions with people of different faiths. Until then, the specifics of those other belief systems weren't demanding our attention.

Then came September 11, 2001. The terrorist attacks on that day brought the religion of Islam into the news reports and conversations of everyone around the world. We were told that a "holy war" had been declared on America and its allies. Certain militant Muslims referred to Americans as *infidels* who must be wiped off the face of the earth according to the teachings of Muhammad. Other Muslims, however, quickly retorted that the attacks were the work of *Islamic fundamentalists* who were perverting the true teachings of Muhammad.

In the midst of America's military response, interesting debates ensued between politicians, theologians, and anyone else with access to a microphone. Is Islam a religion of peace or hostility? Is the God of the Muslims the same as the God of the Christians?

(Is he the same God, just aka Allah?) Questions of this sort led to deeper inquiries. Do the differences between the various religions matter? Aren't there different ways to get to God? How can any group of people claim to have a monopoly on the truth? How should you decide between different religions? Does one size fit all, or can you shop around till you find one that is uniquely tailored to fit your many moods and accommodate your personal proclivities?

Like many people, our intense curiosity about the religion of Islam arose almost overnight. No longer were we content with just a slight familiarity of the Muslim faith. Our questions had *real life* relevance to socio-political events on the evening news. We had to learn more.

## This Book Is for You If...

In the pages that follow, we're going to tell you what we learned from our crash-course study of Islam. We were surprised with some of the similarities Islam shares with the beliefs of Christianity. We were even more surprised with the differences. These

are not just slight differences (like whether you call your place of worship a *church* or a *mosque*). No, for the most part the differences are significant, with eternal ramifications (like the nature of God and what is required to avoid everlasting damnation).

With consequences that crucial, you might think an explanation of Islam requires an expert. Well, we are no experts, but we think that is a good thing. Experts often take a simple subject to a level of incomprehensibility. Not so with us; we've kept it plain and simple. But we have done our homework. We actually read the books written by scholars who *are* experts. We've condensed what they said into a format that makes sense out of complexity. (We guess that makes us the anti-experts.) And even though we bring with us our Christian viewpoint, we'll keep our report objective. We respect the sincerity of the faith that is held by Muslims. It is not our purpose or intent to denigrate or belittle the religion of Islam. But we will make comparisons and contrasts with Christianity to help you identify the distinctions.

So, you are reading the wrong book if you are looking for a comprehensive treatise on the religion of Islam. (The fact that this book isn't hardbound, 600 pages thick, and priced at $75 should have been a clue.) But, this book is for you if…

✓ You are confused about what Islam really teaches.

✓ You want an overview of the beliefs of Islam but don't want to earn a master's degree in comparative world religions in the process.

✓ You want to know how Islam compares with Christianity, but you want to avoid a presentation that is tainted with "Us vs. Them" animosity.

## Parts of This Book Are Marginal

We are confident that you'll find our discussion to be informative, but some of the most helpful information isn't in the text. Instead, you'll find it in the margin. For your reading convenience, we have strategically placed icons in the left margin on the pages throughout the book. They add to the visual variety, but these are not just graphic gratuities. They are intended to help you scrutinize, skim, or skip the text (according to your preference). Memorize them now so you'll recognize them later:

 Big Idea—We know you won't hang on every word we write. So when we say something that absolutely, positively should be read, we'll mark it with this icon.

 Learn the Lingo—There is no need to be intimidated by foreign terminology. We'll give you understandable definitions.

 Glad You Asked—We try to anticipate your question and give you the answer before you ask it.

 Bruce & Stan Say—Most of the time we keep our own opinion to ourselves. But sometimes we can't help from interrupting ourselves. (At least we warn you when it happens.)

 Dig Deeper—At the end of each chapter, we'll give you a list of several books that go into greater detail than what we have discussed.

## A Final Thought

It doesn't matter whether your interest in
Islam is prompted by curiosity, concern, or
calamity. You are doing a good thing to
embark on this study. Knowing the principles of someone else's faith can promote
understanding and friendship with them. It
can also help strengthen your knowledge of
your own faith. It is our prayer that you
experience both of those results from
reading this book.

# CHAPTER 1

## FINDING YOUR RELIGION: WHAT YOU BELIEVE REALLY MATTERS

*You say, there is no religion now.
'Tis like saying, in rainy weather,
there is no sun.*

—Ralph Waldo Emerson

**BRUCE & STAN SAY** Religion is one of the most universal practices in the, well, in the universe. In its most basic form, religion is anything that engages in or interacts with some sort of spiritual reality. Many religious people go to church, mosques, or synagogues. Others meditate privately in a little corner of their room. And some commune with nature on top of a mountain. All would consider themselves religious.

Religion is great, but religious structure by itself—no matter how formal or casual—never gave anybody the answers to the big questions of life (such as "Why am I here?" or "What happens when I die?"). That's why so many people are discouraged by religion. They know there is a spiritual reality "out there," but they can't find any real answers in religion.

That's because it's not the religion that matters; it's what the religion teaches. Or more precisely, it's what the religion *believes.* When it comes to belief, there's only one thing that counts: Is it true? If it's not true, who cares? But if the truth about life is there, then it makes all the difference in the world.

As we embark on this study of Islam, we want to start with some ideas about religion and truth (and we'll tell you the story of Islam in the process). Because what you believe really does matter.

*Bruce & Stan*

# Chapter 1

# Finding Your Religion: What You Believe Really Matters

*What's Ahead*

➤ The Story of Islam
➤ Why Religion?
➤ Let's Find the Truth

*H*ave you ever wondered how a religion gets started? We've wondered:

✓ Do a bunch of people get together and decide to start a church just so they can pass the collection plate and start a television ministry?

✓ Does God look down from heaven and choose someone to start a new belief

system just so he can have a few more
buildings with stained-glass windows
built in his honor?

✓ Does some ambitious person decide to
start a new path to God because he
believes all of the others lead to
nowhere?

Here's one story that may help you understand how a religion gets going. It's the
true account (short version) of the early
beginnings of Islam:

## The Story of Islam

Muhammad ibn Abdallah was born in A.D.
570 into a prominent family in the city of
Mecca, Arabia (now Saudi Arabia). His
father died before he was born, and his
mother died when he was six. Raised by his
uncle, Muhammad married a 40-year-old
wealthy widow named Khadijah when he
was 25. The newlyweds settled in Mecca,
where Muhammad became a successful
businessman.

Compared to the monotheistic belief
systems of Judaism and Christianity, which

were the dominant religions in other parts of the Middle East, the religious traditions practiced by the Arabs were polytheistic and idolatrous. Muhammad rejected the pagan idolatry of his culture, and he came to believe in only one God, Al-Lah, or Allah, a name that means "the God." On a regular basis the thoughtful young man would hike to a cave on the summit of Mount Hira, just outside Mecca, to pray and fast.

## DEFINING THE TERMS

A *monotheistic* religion is one that believes in one God, while *polytheistic* religions believe there are many gods. A *pagan* is someone who does not follow one of the major religions (such as Christianity, Judaism, and Islam).

In 610, when Muhammad was 40 years old, he received the first of a series of mystical visions, or revelations, that changed his life and the world. Initially Muhammad was unsure whether his visions were divine or not, but his wife was convinced they were from God. Eventually Muhammad came to believe the archangel Gabriel delivered God's message directly to him: There was only one God, and idolatry was an abomination.

## ISLAMIC FUNDAMENTALS

The word *Islam* means "submission" in the Arabic language. A *Muslim* is a person who submits to *Allah*, the God of *Muhammad*, the man who founded Islam. *Muhammad* is sometimes spelled *Mohammed* or *Muhammed*, but all of these names refer to the same man. Some people refer to the *Qur'an*, the holy book of Islam, as the *Koran*.

### The Prophet Preaches

For two years after Muhammad received his first visions, he kept quiet. Then in 612, he felt empowered to preach, and he began gaining converts. For the next 20 years, until his death in 632, Muhammad attracted more followers as he continued to receive revelations, which he began to recite for his disciples to write down (Muhammad could not read or write).

Eventually these recitations were collected into a new scripture called the *Qur'an*, which means "the reciting" or "the reading."

The idolatrous and immoral people of Mecca were intensely opposed to Muhammad and his revelations. In 622 Muhammad and a small group of followers were forced to flee north to Yathrib (later renamed Medina, the "city of the prophet").

## THE MIGRATION

Muhammad's migration to Yathrib is known as the flight to Medina, or the *Hegira*. Muslims hold the Hegira in such high regard that the year A.D. 622 marks the beginning of the Islamic calendar. The years since then are counted from "A.H." meaning "the year of the Hegira."

## The Prophet Conquers

Muhammad tried to bring peace to the various tribal groups in Medina, but he was met with resistance. So he organized a small army in order to bring stability to the area. Muhammad built a mosque and formed a government that set rules for the people in all areas of life: religious, economic, political, and social. Meanwhile, back in his hometown, the Meccans organized an army to destroy Muhammad and his followers. But Muhammad turned the tables and conquered Mecca with his band of warriors in A.D. 630. He destroyed every idol in the main temple, except for the *Kabah*, the sacred Black Stone where Muslims believe Abraham was tempted to sacrifice his son, Ishmael. From that time forward the Kabah in Mecca has been the most holy shrine in Islam. This is the place where all Muslims direct their prayers.

For the next two years, Muhammad became the leading prophet and the ruler of Arabia as he governed people in the name and worship of Allah. After Muhammad's death in 632, his followers zealously carried their new faith across Asia, Africa, and into Europe. Today, more than 1 billion people call themselves Muslims.

## Why Religion?

Even though Islam is the world's second most popular religion, it's only one of many. There are 6 billion people on the planet, and four-fifths of them—that's nearly 5 billion of us—practice some kind of religion. And what a huge variety of religious experiences there are! Some people are very casual about their religious practices, while others are zealous for their faith. A few religions teach the concept of one God, but many aren't so sure: There can be many gods or no God; you simply believe in what seems right to you.

A lot of people believe that all religious groups—Christians, Muslims, Mormons, Buddhists, and so on—believe in the same God, only they explain it in different ways. They see God as living at the top of a very big mountain, and all the religions and belief

### The World's Most Popular Religions

*The most popular religious groups in the world are:*

*Christians—2 billion*

*Muslims—1 billion*

*Hindus—800 million*

*Buddhists—300 million*

*More than a billion people worldwide consider themselves atheists or nonreligious.*

systems in the world are like different trails that make their way to the top. Just like every trail eventually reaches the summit, every religion eventually reaches God.

### They Can't All Be True

Well, we respectfully disagree with that explanation for one very simple reason: *All religions cannot be true.* How can we be so sure? Because all religions are different. Each religion has a different concept of God or gods, which would be fine, except that religion did not invent God. God exists apart from us and apart from our religious belief systems. We didn't create God; God created us. If God were merely a feeling or an experience that you could take like some kind of magic pill designed to make you feel good, then it wouldn't make any difference what you believe.

But that's not who God is. He is God, and if you're going to believe in him, then you need to find a religion or a belief system that tells the truth about him. And there's the problem. No two religions are alike. In fact, as Dr. Ravi Zacharias explains, "Every religion is at its core exclusive."

## Let's Find the Truth

At this point you may be wondering: "Doesn't every religion contain some truth?" Absolutely. But that doesn't mean the entire belief system is true. And when it comes to God and your eternal destiny (a pretty important part of any religion, by the way), doesn't it make sense to make sure your beliefs are completely true? After all, this is your life we're talking about here.

That's why we want to do our best to help you sort out the truth by examining your religious and spiritual beliefs, and we're going to do that by comparing Christianity to the religion of Islam. Why narrow it down to just these two religions? First, Christianity and Islam are the world's most popular belief systems. Second, there are a lot of similarities between them. And third, one of the best ways to know more about what you believe is to compare it to what others believe.

Ultimately, you want to know the truth, and you want

> *The reality is that if religion is to be treated with intellectual respect, then it must stand the test of truth, regardless of the mood of the day.*
>
> *—Ravi Zacharias*

to have confidence that what you believe really is true. That's what we're here to help you do. We want to help you find the truth. So let's get started.

## FIVE DOCTRINES OF ISLAM

These are the five beliefs of Islam, sometimes called the five doctrines of the faith. Muslims and Christians share these beliefs, but with differences. In the next five chapters we will deal with these doctrines and discuss the similarities and the differences between Islam and Christianity.

### God

There is only one God, and his name is Allah. The most common creed of Islam is "There is no God but Allah," which is recited daily by Muslims.

### Angels

Angels are the messengers of Allah. Gabriel is the chief angel. There is a fallen angel named Shaitan, as well as followers of Shaitan, called jinns (demons).

## *Sacred Scriptures*

Muslims are known as "people of the book." Muslims believe that Allah has revealed himself through four books: The Torah (God gave this to Moses); the Zabur (the Psalms of David); the Injil (the gospel of Jesus); and the Qur'an, which supersedes all previous writings.

## *Prophets*

Like Christianity, Islam is a prophetic religion. The Qur'an names more than 20 prophets, including six who are held in the highest regard: Adam, Noah, Abraham, Moses, Jesus, and Muhammad. The last and greatest prophet is Muhammad.

## *Last Things*

Islam places great emphasis on the Day of Judgment. On the last day, the dead will be resurrected. Allah will judge all people according to their works, and each person will be sent either to heaven or hell.

## *What's That Again?*

1. Islam is a monotheistic religion begun by the prophet Muhammad, who claimed to receive revelations directly from Allah beginning in A.D. 610.

2. Four-fifths of the world's people are religious. One billion practice Islam.

3. Not all religions are true, because each religion has a different concept of the one true God.

4. When you're dealing with God and your eternal destiny, it's important to make sure your beliefs are completely true.

## *Dig Deeper*

There are so many books written about world religions and Islam that it's hard to know where to start. But you have to start somewhere, so here's a list of resources we found especially helpful.

*So What's the Difference?* by Fritz Ridenour is an absolute classic. First published in 1967, this book has been updated and expanded to cover all the current religions and belief systems.

*Understanding World Religions* by George W. Braswell Jr. is a more technical book but still fairly easy to follow. Dr. Braswell is a Professor of Missions and World Religion, and he takes a very objective view to all religions, especially Islam.

One of Karen Armstrong's main objectives in *Islam: A Short History* is to discourage the overly simplistic belief in the Western world that Islam is just an extreme religion that promotes authoritative government, female oppression, and terrorism.

*Jesus Among Other Gods* by Ravi Zacharias is a terrific book about finding the truth. In the process you will learn about the uniqueness of Christianity.

## Moving On

Belief in the one true God is the central doctrine of both Islam and Christianity. Muslims and Christians share many common beliefs regarding this important topic, but they also disagree on some of

God's personality traits, and they see God differently in the way he relates to humankind. The next chapter will help you sort out these important God things.

# CHAPTER 2

## ALL ABOUT ALLAH:
## IS "GOD" BY ANOTHER NAME THE SAME?

*There is no God but God.*

—The Qur'an

**BRUCE & STAN SAY**

There is a song with lyrics that go something like: "You say *potato* and I say *po-tah-to*. You say *tomato* and I say *to-mah-to*." Okay, so these words aren't the most complicated lyrics you'll ever find, but the point is clear: Different pronunciations don't alter the fact that both people are referring to the same thing. Many things are called by different names. Some people call that piece of furniture in the living room a *couch*; others call it a *sofa*. Your grandparents call it a *divan*.

Different names are also used for the same individual. Consider jolly ol' St. Nick, Kris Kringle, or Santa Claus: However he is described, we're still referring to the same fictional obese, red-suited arctic-dweller who is used as a merchandizing gimmick at Christmastime. Same guy, different names.

What about God and Allah? Is it still just a matter of same guy, different names? Or, is there a difference between the God of Christianity and the Allah of Islam? If they are the same, then the Christian and the Muslim have lots in common and ought to be able to overlook their potato/po-tah-to variances. But if each religion has a distinctly different Supreme Being, then the disparity is very significant because both Christianity and Islam claim to worship the only true God. If it is not "one and the same," then it has to mean "choosing between the two." That's what makes this chapter so intriguing.

*Bruce & Stan*

# Chapter 2

# All About Allah:
# Is "God" by Another
# Name the Same?

## What's Ahead

➤ Abraham's Hat Trick
➤ What's Love Got to Do with It?
➤ You Can't Relate to This
➤ Trinity Identity Crisis

*O*rdinarily, we aren't big fans of the plays of William Shakespeare. We like the murder scenes, but we aren't fond of poetry in iambic pentameter, and we cringe at the sight of men in tights. There is one famous Shakespearian quote, however, that applies to this chapter. It is from act II, scene 3 of *Romeo and Juliet:*

> *What's in a name? That which we call a rose*
> *By any other name would smell as sweet.*

Even we can figure that one out. A thing is a thing regardless of what you call it. And so it is with God. Whether you call him *Lord*, *Heavenly Father*, or *Jehovah* (or *Yahweh*, if you are fluent in Hebrew), he is the same God. What about *Allah?* Is that just another name to add to the list? Don't answer yet.

## Abraham's Hat Trick

It is difficult to start a religion. Very few people can pull it off. Oh, sure, any kook can start a religious group in his garage with a few candles and incense, but these are usually scams designed to avoid taxes or fleece the sheep. When it comes to a legitimate religion that will last for centuries, it takes credibility.

Abraham must have had lots of credibility because he was very successful at the religion starting business. He started three of them. Well, to be more precise, he is viewed as the honorable ancestor of three separate religions: Judaism, Christianity, and Islam. These three religions all trace their heritage through Abraham. Whether you are reading the writings of the Old Testament Hebrew prophets, the epistles of New Testament Christians, or the revelations of Muhammad, each religion refers to its patriarch, Abraham, as the friend of God.

Judaism, Christianity, and Islam are referred to as monotheistic religions because each believes in one God. Since they all believe in one God, and since they all trace their progression through Abraham, then the God of each religion must be the same one, right? Don't answer yet.

Since the God of Islam is Abraham's God, then you would expect Muslims to believe in the existence and preeminence of God as emphasized by Abraham. And that's exactly what they do. Islam is a totally God-centered religion.

- Of the five doctrinal beliefs of Islam (see page 24), the first and foremost deals with the existence and importance of God. Muslims believe that there is only one true God (whose name happens to be Allah).

- In the Five Pillars of Islam (see page 93), the very first duty is the requirement to publicly recite the *Shahadah,* which begins with the phrase: "There is no god but Allah."

Any self-respecting Supreme Being is going to have supernatural powers, and this is another aspect in which the Allah of Islam and the God of Christianity are indistinguishable. With the utterance of the words *Allah akbar* in their daily prayers, Muslims acknowledge that "God is greater than everything." They know him to be all-seeing, all-hearing, all-knowing, and all-powerful. The powers they attribute to Allah are the same as those famous "omni-" attributes of the Christian's God:

✓ Omniscience: all-knowing

✓ Omnipotence: all-powerful

✓ Omnipresence: everywhere at the same time

At least as far as the generic concept of God is concerned, the Allah of Islam doesn't conflict with the God of Christianity (or Judaism, for that matter). So far, so good. They seem to be one and the same. But now let's go a little deeper in our examination. When it comes to the character and nature of God and Allah, significant differences become readily apparent. All of a sudden it becomes clear that Christians and Muslims aren't referring to the same God by two different names.

## What's Love Got to Do with It?

If you were asked to describe a friend, you might start off by listing a few physical characteristics. But height and weight statistics only describe what the person looks like. They don't give any clue about *who* the person is. For that, you'd have to describe your friend's personality.

The same principle applies to God. You don't learn much by trying to describe what he looks like (which is difficult when you are dealing with an invisible Being). Any description of God must deal with his nature and character. It is the personality and character of God that quickly separate the views of the Muslim and the Christian.

Muslims have "99 beautiful names" for Allah (which they must memorize), and each one describes one of Allah's characteristics.

You might be surprised to learn that *love* is absent from this long list of character qualities. The Qur'an doesn't describe Allah as loving. His character is more defined by judgment than by grace, or in terms of power rather than mercy (see Surahs 6:142 and 7:31).

> *The Qur'an contains 114 surahs (chapters) and is approximately four-fifths the length of the New Testament.*

This isn't to say that Allah doesn't love. He loves those who do good (meaning that they do good deeds and adhere to and perform the Five Pillars of Islam). But Allah does not love the person whose bad deeds outweigh the good things he or she has done.

This is where the Allah of Islam and the God of Christianity part company. The God of the Bible is known for his love. That is an essential part of his character. The Bible states God's loving nature in plain and simple language so there is no missing it: God is love (1 John 4:8).

While Allah only loves the lovely (those he deems "good"), the God of the Bible loves those who are unlovely (which would include all of humanity). While God cannot tolerate sin, he loves the sinner. That is the whole point of God's love. We are all sinners (Romans 3:23), yet God loved us as sinners. We don't have to clean up our act before we will be acceptable to him (Romans 5:8).

If anyone ever questions whether there is a difference between Allah and God, tell them love is the answer.

## *You Can't Relate to This*

Both Allah and God are described as being transcendent (meaning that they are above and beyond us in other dimensions of time and space). This characteristic fits with the Muslim concept of Allah as a God who is unknowable and incomprehensible.

- In his book *Who Is the Allah of Islam?* author Abd-al-Masih gives the Muslim view that Allah is "unique, unexplorable, and inexplicable." He flatly states that "Allah cannot be comprehended."

- Similarly, George Houssney writes in *What Is Allah Like?* that humans can never know Allah. They may know about him, but they do not have personal, experiential knowledge of him.

Muslims take offense at the notion that a person can know God. To the Islamic mind, a human ability to know God would make God dependent upon his creation. For this reason, Allah doesn't reveal himself; he reveals his *mashi'at* (desires and wishes), but not himself. Since Muslims believe that people cannot know Allah, they don't try to.

That isn't the way it is with Christians and their God. They believe that they "can know the true God" (1 John 5:20). God is not only transcendent, he is also *immanent* (meaning that his presence and activity are within the world and human nature). This means that God can be seen and known through nature itself (Romans 1:19-20).

But God goes further than that. We aren't limited to a knowledge of him that is restricted by the camouflage of nature. He wants us to know him personally. The Bible gives vivid metaphors for the type of intimate, personal relationship that we can have with God:

- We can know him like sheep know their shepherd (John 10:14);

- We can be connected with him and receive the sustenance of life from him

like a branch receives from the vine
(John 15:5); and

- We can experience a bond with him
  like children have with their father
  (Ephesians 1:5).

Knowledge of God isn't limited to an intellectual understanding of him. It is experiential and results from God living within those who believe in him. To the Christian, knowledge of God is a living relationship with him (1 John 4:13-15).

While the Muslim avoids personal knowledge of Allah, it is the goal of every Christian to know God better (Ephesians 1:16-17, 3:18). For the Muslim, Allah remains mysterious, distant, and unapproachable. For the Christian, God is a heavenly Father with outstretched arms who is anxious to embrace those who come to him.

## Trinity Identity Crisis

Perhaps the greatest difference between the Muslim's and Christian's concept of God involves the concept of the Trinity.

Many Muslims mistakenly believe that Christians worship three gods (which would be *tritheism*). However, this assumption comes from a misunderstanding of the Christian doctrine of the Trinity, which recognizes that there is only *one* God, but that there are three coexisting "Persons" within a unity of God:

✓ There is "God" the Father. This is the "Person" of God who figures so prominently in the Old Testament. It is to God the Father that Jesus Christ prayed.

✓ But Jesus Christ is also God. He is referred to as "the Son of God," not in the sense that he is a lineal descendant of God the Father, but rather that he had the identical nature of God the Father.

✓ The Holy Spirit that indwells and empowers Christians is also God.

When Christians consider the doctrine of the Trinity, they marvel at God's incomprehensible complexity. When Muslims hear the concept of the Trinity, they consider it as heresy. As we will explain further in chapter 4, Muslims believe that Allah could have no "son," and that the concept of the Trinity imposes on the Deity human characteristics of sexual procreation. Furthermore, Islam rejects the notion of a triune God as violating their foundational truth that there is only *one* true God.

There is no Arabic word of "three-in-one" or "threefold," so it may be understandable that a language difficulty creates some mis-understanding of the Trinity. But Islam's rejection of the Trinity is much more than just a linguistic hurdle. The Qur'an specifically attacks the concept. In his book *The Koran Interpreted* A.J. Arberry says that the Qur'an emphasizes that Christians are unbelievers because they accept the historic Christian doctrine of the Trinity. He quotes the Qur'an as saying:

> *They are unbelievers who say, "God is the Third of Three." No god is there but one God. If they refrain not from what they say, there shall afflict those of them that disbelieve a painful chastisement.*

It is as if portions of the Qur'an were inten-tionally written to attack the Christian belief in God as a Trinity. So much for any inkling that Islam's Allah and Christianity's God might be the same.

# *What's That Again?*

1. There is common ground for the Muslim and the Christian. Both believe that there is one true God. Both consider God to be the Supreme Ruler of the universe. Both view Abraham as a patriarch of their religion.

2. But don't ever think that the Allah of Islam is the same as the God of Christianity. They are different in many significant respects.

3. Allah is most often characterized in terms of judgment and power. He loves only those who have shown themselves to be good enough. In contrast, the God of Christianity is the essence of love. His love is for all people, even while they are in their sinful condition.

4. Allah is impersonal and mysterious. Christians believe they can know God and have a personal relationship with him.

5. Muslims reject the concept of the Trinity. The God of the Christians is comprised of the Father, Jesus the Son, and the Holy Spirit.

## Dig Deeper

John Ankerberg and John Weldon give a good overview to Islam (with FAQs) in their *The Facts on Islam*.

Although there is no mention of Allah, there is a good overview about the nature and characteristics of God and the concepts of the Trinity in *Bruce & Stan's® Guide to God*, which was written by two of our favorite authors.

If you are into theology in a big way (and by that we mean a thick book with tiny print), check out Millard J. Erickson's *Christian Theology*. There isn't much about God that isn't in this book.

## Moving On

Now that you've got an overview of the differences between God and Allah, let's take a look at the two holy books of Christianity and Islam: the Bible and the Qur'an. If you want to understand Christianity, you have to know where the Bible came from. If you want to know Islam, you have to know how where the Qur'an came from.

In the next chapter we're going to compare and contrast these two amazing books.

# CHAPTER 3

## HOLY BOOK COMPARISON: ARE THE BIBLE AND THE QUR'AN EQUALLY RELIABLE?

*Trust everyone until you have reason not to.*

—Anonymous

**BRUCE & STAN SAY**

Although many people have told us, "If you guys can write a book, anybody can," you need to know that writing a book isn't as easy as you might think. If you expect people to buy your book, you have to be creative, interesting, and accurate. In general people don't like to read books that are predictable, dull, and filled with errors.

If the standards for good books are this high, imagine how lofty the bar has to be set for a *holy* book. By definition, "holy" means morally and spiritually perfect. A holy book is sacred, and it can come only from a divine Being. The Bible and the Qur'an are the world's best-known and most popular holy books. The Bible says that God is its author, and Islam claims that the Qur'an contains the revelations of Allah.

In the last chapter we distinguished between God and Allah. In this chapter we're going to do the same thing with the two holy books that bear their names.

*Bruce & Stan*

# Chapter 3

# Holy Book Comparison:
# Are the Bible and the
# Qur'an Equally Reliable?

## What's Ahead

➤ How Was the Scripture Written?
➤ How Was the Scripture Recognized as Authoritative?
➤ How Was the Scripture Transmitted to the Present Day?

*E*very one of the major religions has a holy book, sometimes referred to as sacred writings or scriptures. The best-known holy books belong to the three great monotheistic religions: Judaism has the Torah, Christianity has the Bible, and Islam has the Qur'an. All three of these holy books contain the words of their prophets as they spoke the message of God to the people.

In this chapter we're going to focus on the Bible and the Qur'an, specifically to make comparisons between the two holy books. These sacred scriptures play a central role in both religions because they reveal God's nature and how he relates to the world. In this chapter we want to evaluate and make comparisons between these two holy books according to three different criteria.

- How was the Scripture written?

- How was the Scripture recognized as authoritative?

- How was the Scripture transmitted to the present day?

By the time we're done, it should be clear as to which holy book is most reliable and trustworthy.

## How Was the Scripture Written?

A book doesn't just show up one day in your local bookstore. Amazon.com doesn't create the books it sells. A person or some people had to write the book in the first place. It's no different with the Bible and the Qur'an. They had to be written. The question is *how* and *by whom*.

## The Bible

The Bible is often called the Word of God for a very simple reason: That's what it is. The Bible isn't just some words *about* God. The Bible represents the very words of God himself (Hebrews 1:1).

The process God used to write the Bible is referred to as *inspiration,* which literally means to *breathe in.* God breathed his words into 40 different writers over a period of 1500 years through the Holy Spirit (2 Peter 1:21). This idea of God breathing into the human authors is consistent with how God created the universe in the first place (Psalm 33:6). It's also the way God created humanity (Genesis 2:7).

## Proof of the Truth

If God does not (and cannot) lie, and if God wrote the Bible through the divine inspiration of the Holy Spirit, then you can trust the Bible as true (Psalm 33:4).

## PROPHETIC PROOF

Both Christianity and Islam are known as "prophecy" religions because their holy books contain predictions about the future. The Bible is unparalleled for its 100 percent accuracy when it comes to prophecy. Dr. Hugh Ross, a world-renowned astrophysicist, has researched every prophecy. He writes that approximately 2000 of the 2500 prophecies in the Bible have already been fulfilled to the letter with no errors (the remaining 500 concern events that have not yet occurred). The only explanation for this incredible accuracy is that God himself made and fulfilled the prophecies. There is no other possibility.

## The Qur'an

Dr. George Braswell, a scholar in the field of world religions, wrote this about the Qur'an:

> Of the scriptures of all the religions of the world, perhaps the Qur'an is looked upon by its followers as ideally and practically the most holy. Muslims believe that the Qur'an was revealed

to their prophet, Muhammad, in the Arabic language, which is the very language spoken by Allah in heaven. Allah is the author of the Qur'an, and Muhammad is the channel of Allah's word to the people.

The Qur'an includes much of the information from the Bible. More than 20 prophets—including Abraham, Moses, and Jesus—are mentioned. Much of the teaching about God in the Qur'an is consistent with the Bible, such as the belief that God is sovereign. The Qur'an also contains a number of stories that are similar to events from the Jewish and Christian traditions. Islam accepts both Jews and Christians as "people of the book," and it views the Jewish Torah and the Christian Gospels (which Islam calls *Injil*) as Allah's revelation to these pre-Islamic people.

However, Islam teaches that the Torah and the Injil were "misinterpreted" by Jews and Christians. In effect, they were corrupted. Muhammad is the final prophet, and the Qur'an is the final revelation. According to Braswell, Muslims believe that the Qur'an "clarifies and supersedes" God's revelations prior to Islam.

All of the ideas in the Qur'an are credited to Allah, but Muhammad was the only recipient of divine revelation. He did not write down the words he heard. Instead Muhammad dictated part of the Qur'an during the 20 years when he was receiving his revelations, and then the rest of the text came from his followers, who recalled his recitations after he died. Karen Armstrong writes: "Muhammad's successors, however, were not prophets, but would have to rely on their own human insights."

## Proof of the Truth

Since the Qur'an was revealed to Muhammad alone, and then written down by his followers, the trustworthiness of the Qur'an depends on several factors. In his book *The Origins of the Koran*, Ibn Warraq points these out:

- Muhammad had to memorize perfectly what God revealed to him through his angels.

- Muhammad's followers had to hear and understand Muhammad precisely.

- As they wrote down what they heard, the followers had to remember the recitations exactly as Muhammad spoke them.

---

## OTHER IMPORTANT BOOKS OF ISLAM

Although the Qur'an is the final and ultimate authority for all Muslims, there are some other important "written traditions" that serve as guides in faith and practice. *Sunnah* are some sayings of Muhammad that show how he acted while leading his followers. The Sunnah were collected by Muslim scholars into a book called the *Hadith.* The *Shari'ah* is a conduct guide for Muslims. Braswell calls *Qiyas* "the agreement of a Muslim community on an interpretation of the Qur'an and the Hadith."

---

## How Was the Scripture Recognized as Authoritative?

Anyone could claim to be a prophet of God, and anyone could claim to have revelations from God (we once met a guy who said he was Jesus, but only for two weeks). So how did people in the ancient world know the prophets and their writings were for real? There had to be a process for determining authenticity. Let's look at the procedure used for the Bible and the Qur'an.

### The Bible

*Canonicity* was the process early scholars and church leaders used to determine which books of the Bible were inspired by God. The *canon* is the word that describes the 66 books that make up the Bible (the word *canon* comes from the root word *reed*, which was used as a measuring stick in ancient times).

The final book of the Bible to be inspired by God was the book of Revelation. The apostle John, who was the human author, finished writing Revelation at the end of the first century. For the next few hundred years, several church councils met to determine which books should be included in the canon of Scripture. Their main task was to evaluate books written during and after the time of Christ (the Old Testament canon had already been determined). According to Dr. Norman Geisler, a Bible scholar, the councils followed strict guidelines in order to determine whether or not a book was inspired by God. They asked themselves:

1. Does it speak with God's authority?
2. Is it written by a man of God speaking to us as a prophet of God?
3. Does it have the authentic stamp of God?
4. Does it impact us with the power of God?
5. Was it accepted by the people of God?

It is important to know that the canon councils did not *declare* a book to be from God. They simply *recognized* the divine influence that was already there.

## The Qur'an

The entire text of the Qur'an was not completed until after Muhammad's death, because there was always the possibility that fresh revelations could be added while he was still alive. However, when the prophet died, his followers decided to make a collection of the whole Qur'an into a single book.

Islamic tradition holds that many followers, including four men closest to

Muhammad, knew the Qur'an in its entirety during Muhammad's lifetime. A problem arose when a number of tribes recently converted to Islam in the Arabian Peninsula reverted to paganism after Muhammad died. They revolted against Muslim rule, so Abu Bakr, Muhammad's chief successor, sent an army to subdue the rebels. As a result, a number of the followers who knew the Qur'an directly from Muhammad were killed.

Abu Bakr realized there was a danger that the Qur'an might be lost if any more of its most trusted reciters passed away, so he commissioned Zaid ibn Thabit to search for portions of the Qur'an and collect them into a single book. It was a difficult task, because the contents of the Qur'an were widely scattered. There were many followers who had memorized parts of Muhammad's revelations, and there were fragments of the text that had been written down on a variety of materials. Zaid had to put everything together.

Zaid wasn't the only one who was working to collect pieces of the Qur'an into a single text. There were others who claimed to have learned as many as 70 Surahs directly from Muhammad, but Islamic tradition pays special attention to Zaid's work, even though it differs from other collections.

Muslims claim that the Qur'an is an exact representation of Muhammad's revelations "without so much as a dot or stroke ever having been lost, changed, or substituted in any way." John Gilchrist writes:

> This is a strange claim to make for a book which had to be compiled piece-meal from various sources scattered among the companions of Muhammad, particularly in the light of further evidences that some passages have been lost, that others have been abrogated, and that other codices compiled about the same time as Zaid's had numerous readings that differed from his and from each other's.

## How Was the Scripture Transmitted to the Present Day?

*Transmission* here has nothing to do with your car. When it comes to Scripture, it describes the total process of transmitting the sacred writing from the early writers to present-day readers (that's us) using the

most practical and reliable methods
possible. Let's look at the methods used to
transmit the Bible and the Qur'an.

## The Bible

Muslims do not dispute the accuracy of the
Old Testament. It's the New Testament they
have problems with, mainly because of the
Gospels (the biographies of Jesus). Muslims
believe the New Testament documents
were corrupted in their transmission. But
that's just not true. Here are just two
reasons why scholars consider the New
Testament to be a group of documents of
the utmost reliability.

1. An important measurement of
   accuracy and reliability is the number
   of copies that exist. In the original
   Greek alone, more than 5000
   manuscript portions of the New Testament have been preserved. The oldest
   is a manuscript fragment of the
   Gospel of John dating no more than 40
   years after the book was written.

2. Another test of accuracy has to do
   with corroborating evidence. There are
   many other historical documents
   written at the same time as the New

Testament that confirm the claims of the Scripture. Not every person, date, or fact in the Bible has been verified by outside sources, but many have, and not one has been shown to be false.

## The Qur'an

Scholars generally agree that the oldest surviving texts of the Qur'an cannot be dated earlier than 150 years after Muhammad's death. This isn't a problem as far as ancient manuscripts are concerned. The problem is that Muslims typically believe that one or more of Zaid's texts have survived completely intact to the present day. "The motive for this popular belief," writes Gilchrist, "is the desire to prove from existing texts that the Qur'an is unchanged to its last letter from its first written codices down to its most recent copies."

This is an impossible claim, and it's unnecessary. Christians have never made a claim like that for any version of the Bible. The Bible we have today is completely true, but only the original manuscripts recorded by the 40 writers inspired by the Holy Spirit are without error (because God, who is the author, is incapable of error).

The same could be said of the Qur'an, except that Muhammad, who claimed to have received direct revelation from Allah through angels, never wrote the words down. And those followers who did record the recitations of Muhammad never agreed on the complete text. So no matter how you look at it, it's inconceivable that the present Arabic text of the Qur'an is an exact copy of the original.

## WHERE IS THE ORIGINAL QUR'AN?

If Muslims believe that the original Qur'an has survived intact, then where is it? Muslims say that the original Arabic Qur'an is in heaven (according to Islam, Arabic is the language of heaven). No authorized translations of the Qur'an into English have ever been produced. Gilchrist writes: "Virtually every English version has been the work of only one man, whether done by Muslim scribes or by Orientalists in the West. As a result, each translation to some extent reflects the bias of the writer no matter how sincerely he may have attempted to produce a text as close to the Arabic original as he can."

## *What's That Again?*

1.  The Bible is important to Christianity and the Qur'an is important to Islam because they both reveal God's nature and God's relation to the world.

2.  God wrote the Bible through the Holy Spirit, inspiring 40 writers to record the text. The Qur'an was revealed to Muhammad, who recited his revelations to various followers.

3.  Canonicity was the process scholars used to recognize which books of the Bible were inspired by God. The Qur'an was collected by various "reciters." The most trusted text was compiled by Zaid ibn Thabit.

4.  Muslims claim the New Testament was corrupted, but a wide range of scholars disagree. Muslims claim the Qur'an is perfect, but no evidence for that claim exists.

## *Dig Deeper*

The issue of scriptural reliability is absolutely crucial as we compare Christianity and Islam. Here are some books that explore this subject more.

Believe it or not, we found *Bruce & Stan's®️ Guide to the Bible* and *Bruce & Stan's®️ Pocket Guide to Studying Your Bible* to be very helpful (and we think you will too).

*Reasonable Faith* by William Lane Craig is an excellent book on Christian truth and apologetics. We focused on the chapter on the historical reliability of the New Testament.

*The Origins of the Koran,* edited by Ibn Warraq, contains some classic essays on Islam's holy book written over the last 150 years.

*The Qur'an: The Scripture of Islam* by John Gilchrist, and *The Qur'an and the Bible in Light of History and Science* by William F. Campbell are both extremely technical. Even though we used them in our research (we did it for you), don't feel like you have to read them.

## Moving On

A central belief of Islam is that the Bible—in particular the New Testament—was corrupted, while the Qur'an is perfect, and as such supersedes the Bible as God's final revelation. We have shown that neither of these claims is true. However, we don't believe that diminishes the importance of the Qur'an, and it doesn't change the fact that the Qur'an represents the essential teachings of Muhammad. In the next chapter, we're going to continue to examine those teachings as they apply to the person of Jesus, the central focus of Christianity.

# CHAPTER 4

## WHO ARE THOSE GUYS?: THE SIGNIFICANCE OF MUHAMMAD AND JESUS

*Is-lam (n.) the religion in which the chief prophet and founder is Mohammed*

*Chris-ti-an-ity (n.) the religion based upon belief in Jesus and upon his teachings*

—Webster's New World College Dictionary

If you haven't done so, please read the dictionary definitions of Islam and Christianity that are printed on the other side of this page. Now, think about this: Islam has a founder, but Christianity doesn't. Don't you find that strange?

Here is another bizarre twist. The religion of Islam considers Jesus to be one of its prophets, yet he lived 500 years before the birth of Muhammad, the founder of Islam. How could Jesus know about a religion that hadn't been invented yet?

There's more. Muhammad revered Jesus, and so do all other Muslims. But Christians consider Muhammad's theology to be heresy. Moreover, Jesus has a significant role in Islam, but Muhammad is irrelevant in the history of Christianity. Does this make sense?

And what about this: You can't believe the statements of *both* Jesus and Muhammad because what each one said contradicts the other. Thus, the interface between Muhammad and Jesus becomes an interesting one. What you believe about each one will determine whether you consider Islam or Christianity to be believable. That's what makes this chapter worthy of your consideration.

*Bruce & Stan*

# Chapter 4

# Who Are Those Guys?: The Significance of Muhammad and Jesus

## What's Ahead

➤ Islam—Prioritizing Your Prophets
➤ Christianity—What a Difference a Deity Makes

For about 2000 years, people have been debating whether Jesus Christ was God or human. The question of *deity vs. man* has never been asked with respect to Muhammad. As far as everyone is concerned—whether Muslim, Christian, or agnostic—Muhammad was mortal. And there is skeletal dust in his grave to prove it.

The question of Christ's deity or humanity is not exclusively relevant to Christianity. It has ramifications for Islam as well.

According to the revelations received by Muhammad as reported in the Qur'an, Jesus was not God. But the Bible says that he was. As we will discuss in the next chapter, the Qur'an quotes Muhammad as saying that salvation is obtained through specified behavior, but the Bible records the statements of Jesus that salvation comes through faith in him as God. In this context, the dichotomy between the theology of Christians and Muslims has eternal significance.

Since your eternal destiny may depend upon it, perhaps we ought to examine the claims about Muhammad and Christ. Let's start with how each is viewed by Islam, and then we'll look at how each is considered in the doctrine of Christianity.

# *Islam—Prioritizing Your Prophets*

Bottom line: Muslims don't think that there is much difference between Jesus and Muhammad. They were both prophets of Islam. But Muhammad came later, and he was the new and improved prophet who outranked Jesus.

## *What Goes Into Making a Prophet?*

Muslims agree with Christians that there was a lot of hoopla surrounding the birth of Jesus (Mary being a virgin, the angels, the

star, etc.). There were no such distinguishing features present when Muhammad was
born. Consequently, there is no claim that
he was anything other than a normal
human being. No divine heritage. No
superpowers. In fact, it is a major tenet of
the Islamic faith that Muhammad was
merely mortal (with imperfections and sin).
As Muhammad himself said:

*I am but a man like you* (Surah 41:6).

### DID YOU KNOW?

Christians don't want the humanity
of Jesus to overshadow his divinity;
if you have the former without the latter, then
Christianity falls apart. With Islam, the
problem is just the opposite, as Muslims are
tempted to exalt Muhammad to almost god-
like status above and beyond his role as
Islam's mortal prophet. In certain parts of the
Islamic world (mostly North Africa and
Southeast Asia), there is a big celebration on
Muhammad's birthday. But in Arabia, and
among Muslims who follow the predominant
interpretation of Islamic law, celebrating the
birthday of Muhammad is forbidden and
considered unlawful.

The only distinguishing and exceptional features of Muhammad were his designation as the principal prophet for Allah and his devotion and faithfulness. His role as a prophet of Islam cannot be understated. Muslims believe that Allah has sent 124,000 prophets to proclaim the Islamic message (with more than 20 of them being specifically mentioned by name in the Qur'an), and Muhammad is considered the greatest of them all.

The list of other prophets isn't too shabby. You'll recognize a few names of the list: Adam, Noah, Abraham, Moses, David, Solomon, Jonah, John the Baptist, and Jesus. Each of these prophets is believed to have brought Allah's truth to the prophet's particular time and culture, but Muhammad is considered a prophet for all time. His message preempts and supersedes all others. His universal, definitive, and conclusive message is recognized by his designation as "the Seal of the Prophets" (Surah 30:40).

## Taking Jesus off the Pedestal

Muslims view Jesus as a very important prophet, just not as important as Muhammad.

As such, followers of the Islamic faith honor Jesus, but not any more than any other prophet (and less than Muhammad).

Interestingly, Muslims believe that Jesus Christ was sinless. Not even Muhammad has this distinction. And the Qur'an even teaches that Jesus was born of a virgin:

> *(And remember) when the angels said: O Mary! Lo! Allah giveth thee glad tidings of a word from Him, whose name is the Messiah, Jesus, son of Mary, illustrious in the world and in the Hereafter, and one of those brought near (unto Allah). He will speak unto mankind in his cradle and his manhood, and he is of the righteous. She said: My Lord! How can I have a child when no mortal hath touched me? He said: So (it will be). Allah createth what he will. If he decreeth a thing, He saith unto it only: Be! and it is* (Surah 3:345-47).

Christians point to these characteristics of Christ as proof of his deity. But not Muslims. They don't make a connection between Christ's distinctives (such as his perfection and virgin birth) and with him being God in human form. Muslims consider that his only relationship with God was as a messenger. They refuse to recognize him as "the Son of

God." It is blasphemy to a Muslim to suggest that Jesus could be God, and the Qur'an emphatically denies it:

> *They do blaspheme who say: "God is Christ the son of Mary....Christ the son of Mary was no more than an apostle"* (Surah 5:73, 78).

It is easy to understand how Muslims see sacrilege in the claim that Jesus was God. As William J. Saal explains in *Reaching Muslims for Christ*, the ordinary Muslim may rationalize the heavenly Father-Son relationship like this:

> First of all, what is the meaning of "Father"? "Father" means that he married and sired children. And marriage is an animal function. And you claim that God is "the Father." So God is an animal?!

Of course, the reference by Christians to Jesus being "the Son of God" is intended as a designation of his deity. It is never intended to suggest that God had sexual relations or that Christ was the birth child of God. But even if a Muslim moves beyond the semantics, the notion of God the Father and God the Son flies in the face of the Islamic doctrine of the singularity of God. To suggest that there are partners or companions to Allah, or that he has co-gods, is considered "the one unforgivable sin" (referred to as *shirk*).

> **Did You Know?**
>
> *Because Christians insult Allah with their polluted concepts (such as Jesus being Allah's son), the Qur'an recommends that Muslims refrain from making friends with Christians (Surah 5:51). It also instructs Christians to maintain a low social profile and enjoy the protection of the Islamic community (Surah 9:29).*

For the Christian, the greatest proof that Christ was God is found in his crucifixion, death, resurrection, and ascension. Interestingly, Islam proclaims that Jesus ascended to heaven, but Muslims deny the prior events in the sequence. According to the doctrines of Islam, Jesus did not die on the cross (Judas was crucified in his place), so there was no death (according to the predominant Muslim viewpoint) and, consequently, no resurrection.

## Christianity—What a Difference a Deity Makes

The preceding few pages profiled Muhammad and Jesus from a Muslim's viewpoint. Now let's look at those same two individuals from the perspective of a Christian. As we did before, we'll start with Muhammad.

## Was Muhammad Running a Non-Prophet Organization?

The Christian and the Muslim are agreed about so many things concerning Muhammad:

- He was born a mortal.

- He lived a mortal life (with sin and imperfections).

- He was a very religious person.

- He was sincere and passionate about his beliefs.

- He died and was buried (and he hasn't been seen or heard from since).

The only aspect of Muhammad's life about which Muslims and Christians disagree is whether or not he was a true prophet of the true God. On this issue, Muslims say, "Without a doubt!" Christians respond: "Not a chance!"

When Muslims argue about this issue with Christians, they rely on several verses to support their position that Muhammad is mentioned in the Bible. In each of these situations, however, it is a big stretch to make Muhammad fit into the verse. For example:

✓ In Deuteronomy 18:15-18, Moses referred to a future prophet. Muslims say that the "future prophet" is a reference to Muhammad. Christians argue that the verse refers to Jesus because it mentions that the prophet will be an Israelite (not an Arab, like Muhammad).

✓ Muslims also cite several New Testament passages (such as John 14:16; 16:7-8) in which Jesus told his disciples that "the Counselor" would come after him. Muslims identify the "the Counselor" as Muhammad. The word *Counselor* in these verses is sometimes translated "Comforter." (It comes from the Greek word *paraclete*.) Muslims say that Muhammad is that "Counselor" because the Qur'an at Surah 61:6 refers to him as Allah's *periclytos* (meaning "praised one"). But this is not a case of a word that was erroneously transcribed as *paraclete* instead of *periclytos*. These are two separate and distinct words with different meanings, and more than 5300 transcripts of the New Testament used the word *paraclete* in these verses (never the word *periclytos*). But there is even stronger evidence that these verses are not referring to Muhammad. Instead, the context of each of these verses cited clearly and specifically identifies the Holy Spirit as "the Counselor." Read them for yourself and see what you think.

> **But Look At the Good Side**
>
> *Although Christians don't recognize Muhammad as a prophet of God, they can appreciate his great historical significance. Beyond mere fame, Muhammad has had a beneficial influence in society because he preached a message of repentance.*

According to the Christian viewpoint, Muhammad wasn't a true prophet of God. If he didn't speak for God, then his words shouldn't be relied upon as truth—especially as they pertain to matters of salvation.

## *All Signs Point to God*

As we mentioned previously, there are certain things about Jesus on which Muslims and Christians are in agreement. They just don't agree on the significance. For example:

- the fact that he was born of a virgin

- his ability to perform miracles

Muslims don't see these things as proof of Christ's deity, but Christians do.

While Muslims and Christians are agreed on the facts surrounding Christ's birth and life, they are in disagreement about the end of his life. Muslims don't acknowledge the crucifixion because it is inconceivable to them that Allah would permit one of his prophets to be killed. But the crucifixion of Jesus and his subsequent resurrection are two fundamental principles of the Christian faith. Christians consider them to be undeniable and unavoidable.

Christianity is all about Jesus being God. As we'll explain in the next chapter, if Jesus was not God, then he wasn't perfect. If he wasn't perfect, then his death wouldn't be effective to pay the penalty for our sin. If our sins aren't covered by his death, then we don't have eternal salvation through faith in him. Christians are counting on him to be God.

The Muslim agrees that Jesus was a great man of God and a prophet who spoke the words of God. But that is not enough for the Christian. The faith of a Christian is premised on the fact that Jesus was God, and that his God-nature empowered him to rise from the dead following his crucifixion. The divergence of views between Islam and Christianity all boil down to one issue: Was Jesus God? If he wasn't, then Muslims are correct in treating him as just another ordinary prophet. But if Jesus was God in the flesh, then he is exactly who he said he was: *the* way, *the* truth, and *the* life, and no one can come to God except through him (John 14:6).

## *What's That Again?*

1. Muslims believe in Jesus, but they consider him to be only a prophet.

2. Muslims also believe Muhammad is the greatest of all Islamic prophets, and his message supersedes anything said by Jesus to the contrary.

3. Muslims deny that Jesus was the Son of God.

4. Although Muslims believe that Muhammad qualifies for some of the prophetic references in the Bible, Christians deny such interpretations. References in the New Testament to "the Comforter" are always referring to the Holy Spirit, not Muhammad.

5. Christianity is premised on the fact that Jesus was God, and Jesus displayed evidence for proof of that fact.

6. Contrary to Islam's denial of the crucifixion and resurrection of Jesus, the Christian religion is based on the truth of these events.

## Dig Deeper

In another shameless plug, let us suggest *Bruce & Stan's® Pocket Guide to Knowing Jesus* by you-know-who. We actually think that you will find it to be a good overview about Jesus.

For information and a quick summary about Muhammad, you also might want to check out a handy brochure: *Islam: What You Need to Know* by Ron Rhodes. It is part of a "quick reference guide" series on religions and other theological issues.

If you are more into an encyclopedia presentation, we found *The HarperCollins Dictionary of Religion* to have an excellent and extensive article about Islam.

## Moving On

As we said at the beginning of this chapter, you can't believe the statements of *both* Jesus and Muhammad because what each one said contradicts the other. Ordinarily, we tend to ignore people who are making contradictory statements about each other (especially during election campaigns). But in this case, we are dealing with individuals who are the focal points of major religions.

It is a big deal that the statements made by Muhammad contradict what Jesus said about himself. But to make matters even

more serious, their conflicting statements
involve the way in which you can obtain
eternal salvation. That particular issue is
the subject of the next chapter.

# CHAPTER 5

## SIN AND SALVATION: YOU CAN'T HAVE ONE WITHOUT THE OTHER

> *The whole conception of "Sin"*
> *is one which I find very puzzling,*
> *doubtless owing to my sinful nature.*
>
> —Bertrand Russell

A lot of things were meant to go together: love and marriage, peanut butter and jelly, Batman and Robin, Bruce and Stan. Then there's sin and salvation. Not exactly on par with a popular song, a kid's sandwich, a pair of superheroes, and a couple of saps, but a whole lot more important.

The reason sin and salvation were meant to go together is that they are mutually exclusive: You really can't have one without the other. If there were no sin in the world, there would be no need for salvation, because you don't need saving unless your life is in danger (and sin does that to you ultimately). And if there were no possible way to be saved, then sin would have its way and we would all be doomed (sorry to get so gloomy).

But there *is* sin in the world (that's the bad news), and there *is* salvation (that's the good news). The question is, how bad is the sin? And how do we get saved? That's what we're going to look at in this chapter as we continue to look at Islam.

*Bruce & Stan*

# Chapter 5

# Sin and Salvation: You Can't Have One Without the Other

*What's Ahead*

➤ Sin: Our Problem
➤ Salvation: God's Solution
➤ Acceptance: Our Response

People who live as if God doesn't matter don't consider sin to be a big deal. They take the approach that you can pretty much do what you want as long as nobody gets hurt. And if you happen to do something that hurts someone or makes you feel guilty, just do something good to make up for it.

People who live as if God does matter take sin very seriously, and this includes Christians and Muslims. They believe that sin separates us from a holy God, who is perfect. The question is, how do we deal with our sin? Even more to the point, how does God deal with it? Does he have a prescription for the sin sickness of the human race, and if he does, how do we respond?

These are the topics we want to talk about in this chapter: sin (our problem), salvation (God's solution to our problem), and acceptance (our response to God's solution). Both Christianity and Islam have a lot in common in some of the areas these topics cover, and in others they are far apart. Let's take a look at how they compare.

## Sin: Our Problem

Anybody who doubts that sin is a problem in our world needs a quick dose of reality:

- ✓ There's a destructive legacy of sin in the events of history (wars, racial hatred, oppression, injustice).

- ✓ There's evidence of sin reported every day in the news (murders, robberies, rapes, cheating).

- ✓ If we're honest, we see the evidence of sin in our own lives (hatefulness, lies, pride, jealousy).

So where did sin come from? Let's take a look at what Christianity and Islam have to say.

## *Christianity*

The Bible teaches that God created Adam and Eve, the first humans, as sinless people. They were in perfect harmony with God and with each other. God could have made Adam and Eve so that they had no choice but to obey and love him, but that's not what he wanted. God created people so that they could *freely* obey and love him (what good is love if it's forced?). This freedom of choice meant that Adam and Eve could freely choose to sin or not sin.

Unfortunately for Adam and Eve (and for us), they chose to disobey God by eating of the fruit God had specifically asked them not to eat. They chose to believe Satan's lie rather than God's truth.

The Bible says that by that one act of rebellion against God, sin entered the entire human race from that time forward (Romans 5:12). Theologians call this dark day "the Fall." It was the day humankind fell out of favor with God to the consequence of sin, which is death (Romans 6:23).

This "death penalty" affected the entire human race in two ways: There was *natural death,* or death of the physical body (Romans 5:12-14), and there was *spiritual death* in that our eternal spirit has been separated from God (Ephesians 2:12).

### Is Man Responsible?

Because of the original sin of Adam and Eve, all of us are affected in two critical ways:

- **We inherit a sin nature.** The sin nature is so corrupt and so pervasive that a parent (no matter how good) can't give birth to anything but a sinful child (no matter how cute).

- **We carry a sin debt.** Sin is directly charged against us—like a bad debt— because when Adam sinned, we sinned (theologians call this "imputed sin").

### Islam

It is important to remember that for the Muslim, everything begins with Allah. *Islam* means "submission," and the Muslim is one who submits to Allah and obeys him.

The greatest sin in Islam is idolatry, or *shirk,* which is giving to anybody or anything even a tiny piece of Allah's unique sovereignty.

So how does Islam view the origin of sin? The Qur'an describes the Fall in much the same way the Bible does: Adam and Eve were created and placed in a beautiful garden and were allowed to eat any fruit they wanted except the fruit of one tree they could not touch (Surah 2:35). Satan tempted Adam and Eve, and they sinned. Their rebellion against Allah and his holy will had a devastating effect on the entire human race. All people were affected by the Fall.

## *Is Man Responsible?*

Muslims believe that man has a moral weakness rather than a sinful nature. He was kicked out of the Garden, but man is not separated from God. According to Abdiyah Akbar Abdul-Haqq, some Islamic traditions teach that a child is born "naturally inclined toward the true religion, which is understood to be Islam." In other words, every child is born a Muslim naturally, but is perverted after birth by his environment. Muhammad is reported to have said that every infant is born "on God's plan," but then his parents make him a Jew or a Christian.

## PEOPLE OF THE BOOK

Although Muslims are convinced that their way is best, they recognize Jews and Christians as "people of the book." The Qur'an encourages all to "strive together (as in a race) towards all that is good" (Surah 2:148). However, Muslims believe there is no spiritual salvation for followers of false religions.

## Salvation: God's Solution

"Salvation" might just be the most important spiritual word any of us will ever hear, because salvation describes how we can be "saved" from the death penalty of our sin to eternal life with God. How does it happen? Well, it's not by accident. God has a definite plan to save us from the eternal consequence of our sin. Let's see how Christianity and Islam present God's solution to our sin problem.

## Christianity

One of the best ways to understand the biblical concept of salvation is to clear up some false ideas about how a person can be saved.

1.  **You are not saved by doing good.** Good deeds are important, and God expects us to do them, but they are meaningless as far as salvation is concerned (Isaiah 64:6). There's nothing a sinful person can do to earn the favor of a perfect God.

2.  **You are not saved by being religious.** Living religiously doesn't bring salvation; God does through his mercy (Titus 3:5).

3.  **You are not saved by being an American.** No nation owns God or Christianity in any special way. Salvation through Jesus Christ is available equally to all people everywhere (Colossians 3:11).

4.  **You are not saved because your parents are Christians.** While *sin* is inherited, *salvation* is not. The decision to accept or reject Jesus is an individual

one (John 1:12-13). Remember, God has lots of children, but no grandchildren.

5. **You are not saved simply because you believe God exists.** When the Bible talks about believing in Jesus, it means more than intellectual understanding. Faith is more than an act of the mind. It requires an attitude of the heart and a commitment of the will.

So if salvation doesn't come from anything we can do, how can we be saved? The Bible teaches that it all comes from God, offered to us as a free gift. It's called *grace,* and it means that we get something—forgiveness of sins and eternal life—even though we don't deserve it (Ephesians 2:8-9).

## *Islam*

Islam also teaches salvation by faith, but with one added feature: good deeds. Despite their unwavering belief in the sovereignty of Allah and his ability to save, Muslims believe in the necessity of contributing to the salvation process with works, but not just any works. To a Muslim, good deeds must be compatible with the teaching of the Qur'an and Hadith.

Like Christianity, Islam views sin as a debt. But rather than asking God to forgive the debt by faith in Jesus Christ, Islam teaches that people must "discharge the debt" by doing good. Allah forgives sins, but there are conditions that must be met. This is why the Five Pillars of Faith are so important in Islam. The Muslim must practice these duties in order to gain paradise.

> *The word* salvation *occurs only once in the Qur'an (Surah 40:44). The idea is that you are delivered from the results of sin by obedience to Allah. Since sin in the Qur'an comes from a moral weakness rather than a sinful nature, salvation does not include the biblical concept of the new birth, also known as regeneration.*

## *The Five Pillars of Islam*

1. *The Confession of Faith (Shahada)* is the first duty of the Muslim. It goes: "There is no God but Allah; Muhammad is the apostle of Allah."

2. *Prayer* is the discipline most consistent Muslims practice because it shows obedience to Allah. Prayer is a ritual carried out five times a day: at dawn,

noon, midafternoon, after sunset, and at night. Prayers, which must be said facing the holy city of Mecca in Saudi Arabia, can be done at home or in the mosque or any convenient place, except for Friday, the Muslim holy day. On that day at noon Muslims go to the mosque to pray as a community.

3. *Giving alms* is generally linked with prayer as the mark of the true believer. The money is given to the poor, orphans, and travelers. Often Muslims will give money to the Ulama, who are the keepers of the legal and religious traditions of Islam. They use gifts to pay the salaries of Muslim clerics, to build and maintain mosques and schools, and to support Muslim missionaries.

4. *Fasting* can be either an expression of piety or penance. It is observed each year during the month of Ramadan, the ninth month of the Muslim calendar (that same month Muhammad first received the revelation of the Qur'an). Fasting Muslims abstain from food, drink, and pleasures from sunrise to sunset each

day (meals may be eaten from sunset until dawn).

5.  *The Pilgrimage to Mecca (hajj)* is the dream of every Muslim. The Qur'an requires that all Muslims travel to Mecca once during their lifetime, although exceptions are made for the sick or those who cannot afford it. Each year during the twelfth month of the Muslim year, millions of the faithful descend on Mecca to accomplish the prescribed rituals, which include paying vows and circling the Kabah, the sacred black stone contained in a cube-shaped shrine. To Muslims, the hajj is symbolic of the global unity of Islam and represents everyone's equality before Allah.

## WHAT'S JIHAD ALL ABOUT?

*Jihad*, or holy war, is a religious duty sometimes associated with the five pillars. At face value, *jihad* requires men to go forth to spread Islam or defend it against infidels. But there are other meanings as well. *Jihad* can mean holy efforts on behalf of Allah, such as becoming a missionary. However, there have been times throughout history (starting with Muhammad) when Muslim leaders have declared holy war against the enemies of Islam, although *jihad* is often justified only in defense of the Islamic community. One who dies in a *jihad* is guaranteed eternal life in paradise.

## *Acceptance: Our Response*

For both Christianity and Islam, it's not enough to recognize God's solution for our problem of sin. We must respond by accepting the plan God has revealed through the sacred Scripture.

### *Christianity*

For Christians, accepting means simply receiving God's offer of salvation through Jesus Christ. All that is required is belief, or faith, that Jesus Christ accepted the death penalty and paid the debt for sin by dying on the cross. The essence of Christian salvation can be summed up in the most famous verse in the Bible:

> *For God so loved the world that he gave his only Son, so that everyone who*

*believes in him will not perish but have eternal life* (John 3:16).

This verse contains a four-step invitation to understand what it means to be saved:

1. **"For God so loved the world"**—Even though we have rebelled against God, he loves us anyway.

2. **"That he gave his only Son"**—Because of our sin, God sent his Son, Jesus Christ, to die a painful death on the cross to pay the price and erase the debt for our sins (Romans 5:8).

3. **"So that everyone who believes in him"**—Accepting salvation requires a conscious step of faith on our part. We must believe that Christ's death and resurrection is all we need to save us, and then we must personally receive Jesus as our Lord and Savior (Romans 10:9).

4. **"Will not perish but have eternal life"**—Without salvation through Jesus Christ, we will spend eternity in hell. With salvation through Jesus, we have new lives—spiritually on this

earth, and eternally in heaven
(Romans 6:23).

## *Islam*

For Muslims, acceptance means *doing* as
well as *believing*. But it doesn't guarantee
forgiveness of sins. One of the interesting
aspects of Islam is that all major sins can be
forgiven only in the hereafter. That's why
the Qur'an emphasizes guidance and
instruction in this life but doesn't talk much
about God changing people on the inside.

In order to ensure salvation and the
forgiveness of sins, the Muslim must pay
back his sin debt by following the
conditions set forth in the Qur'an (such as
the Five Pillars of Faith). But even when
these conditions are met, forgiveness
remains a future hope. And there's no
assurance of salvation, because the forgiveness of Allah depends entirely on his
arbitrary will.

The Bible teaches that all people are sinful,
yet all are free to accept God's offer of salvation. The Qur'an favors determinism. Salvation is a gift of Allah only to those who are
predestined for it. "It is independent of any

moral change in the believer himself,"
writes Abdul-Haqq. "It is *having* rather
than *becoming*."

---

# What's That Again?

1. Both Christians and Muslims take sin very seriously, because sin separates us from God.

2. The Bible teaches that the original sin of Adam and Eve caused the natural and spiritual death of all humankind. Each person inherits a sin nature and carries a sin debt.

3. The Qur'an teaches that man's sin comes from a weakness rather than a sin nature.

4. Christians believe that there's nothing we can do to earn salvation; it is God's gift that must be received by faith.

5. The Muslim view of salvation involves works as well as faith. To pay Allah back for the sin debt, Muslims must meet certain conditions, such as practicing the Five Pillars of Faith.

6. The Bible teaches that all people are free to accept God's offer of salvation. The Qur'an favors determinism.

## Dig Deeper

Abdiyah Akbur Abdul-Haqq has written a very helpful and practical book called *Sharing Your Faith with a Muslim.* Because of his own background, he understands the Muslim mind and the teachings of the Qur'an like few other authors we encountered.

Phil Parshall makes some excellent comparisons between Christianity and Islam in his book, *Inside the Community: Understanding Muslims Through Their Traditions.*

Another book by John Gilchrist is *The Christian Witness to the Muslim.* His observations about the Islamic views of salvation were very valuable to us.

## Moving On

There's one more part to the belief systems of Christianity and Islam, and it's a very important ingredient. What happens when you die? No matter what you believe, if you have no hope for the future, then it isn't worth believing. In the next chapter we're going to talk about death and the afterlife, but don't worry, it isn't at all spooky.

# CHAPTER 6

## DEATH & BEYOND: JUDGMENT & ETERNITY IN THE AFTERLIFE

*In the Day of Judgment they whose balances shall be heavy with good works, shall be happy; but they whose balances shall be light, are those who shall lose their souls, and shall remain in hell forever.*

—Qur'an, Surah 23:104-105

**BRUCE & STAN SAY**

Most major religions—at least all of the ones that involve some sort of god—have a belief in "life after death." After all, if there is no eternity to worry about when a flat line appears on your heart monitor, then all of your religious activities during life won't matter for much.

If you know much about Christianity, we think you'll find a lot that is familiar to you in this chapter. Islam holds to a belief in heaven and hell, and the images are similar to how a Christian might describe them.

This chapter will also cover the sometimes-intimidating subject of the Judgment Day. We'll be talking about the real thing (not a movie with Arnold Schwarzenegger).

We think this chapter will be of interest to you. Maybe not the dying part, but the "Where will you spend eternity?" part.

*Bruce & Stan*

# Chapter 6

# Death & Beyond: Judgment & Eternity in the Afterlife

. . . . . . . . . . . . . . . . . . . . . . . . . . . . . . . . . . . . . . . . . .

## What's Ahead

➤ There Is No Avoiding the "D" Word
➤ Everybody Up! It's Time to Rise and Shine!
➤ Heaven Is High and Hell Is Low

. . . . . . . . . . . . . . . . . . . . . . . . . . . . . . . . . . . . . . . . . .

*A*s you read (and hopefully remember) from chapter 5, Islam (like Christianity) is centered on a concept of salvation. For the Muslim, salvation comes primarily from good deeds (especially faithful practice of the Five Pillars of Islam and adherence to the doctrines of Islam).

Salvation implies that you are saved *from* something. Duh. As you might have suspected, that something is hell. Under Islamic doctrine (like Christianity), hell is a place that you'll want to avoid. Salvation not only excuses you from hell, but it also entitles you to enter heaven. Whether you are a Muslim or a Christian, heaven is a great place to spend eternity (especially given the alternative).

## *There Is No Avoiding the "D" Word*

Bruce is a probate lawyer, so he spends a major portion of his workday dealing with dead-people stuff. He has noticed that most people try to avoid using the word "death." In its place, you might hear terminology such as:

- pass away
- go to the great beyond
- expire
- keel over
- meet the Lord
- kick the bucket
- bite the big burrito

Whatever you call it, death is certain, and everyone has to deal with it.

In the Christian faith, there are not any set rules or protocols for the funeral and burial. Every family does their own thing. Some hold a memorial service; others choose to have a graveside gathering. Some funeral services have an open casket; others don't. You get the idea. You just choose whatever.

Not so with members of the Islamic faith. For them, there are strict procedures that must be followed in every detail. It even starts before death:

- ✓ A dying person is not supposed to be left alone. Family and friends are supposed to gather and pray for forgiveness for the dying person's errors in life.

- ✓ The body of the dying person is to be positioned so that he or she is facing Mecca.

- ✓ Muslims who are about to die must repeat the *Shahada* (the profession of faith): "There is no god but Allah and Muhammad is his messenger." These should be the person's last dying words.

- ✓ Immediately following death, the body is given a bath and wrapped in

> white linen (three layers for a man, five layers for a woman).

✓ The funeral procedure includes a formal "death prayer" that is spoken while the mourners face Mecca in three rows behind the body.

✓ Only males are permitted to bury the body. In the grave, the corpse must be positioned on its right side with the face turned toward Mecca. Dirt is tossed over the body while a passage about resurrection is recited from the Qur'an: "We created you from it and deposit you into it, and from it will take you out once more" (Surah 20:55).

Muslim graves are supposed to be plain and simple. There should be no flowers at the gravesite. A simple pillar can be used to serve as the grave marker. The graves are supposed to point toward Mecca. People are not supposed to visit the gravesite to mourn; instead, they are to use the occasion as a reminder of their own mortality.

*Muslim burial customs can vary according to the region, but cremation is universally forbidden on the grounds that the dead body must be respected and in no way harmed.*

## *Everybody Up! It's Time to Rise and Shine!*

Muslims, like Christians, don't consider physical death as the end. There is more to life after death. (Why do you think it is called the *afterlife?*)

Muslims have a belief that everyone who has ever lived will be resurrected from the dead at some unknown future time. Allah will recreate each individual's body and rejoin his or her soul to it. According to the Qur'an, Allah is leading the events of the world to the day of the resurrection of the dead:

> *It is He who begins (the process of) creation; then repeats it; and for Him it is most easy* (Surah 30:27).

Only Allah knows when the resurrection of the dead will occur. As you might expect, there is a purpose behind all of this. The resurrection is a predicate to the great Day of Judgment. (You can't go on trial if you are still underground.)

**GLAD YOU ASKED**

## WHAT HAPPENS WHEN YOU DIE?

Does anything happen between death and the day of the great resurrection?

> Good question. Muslim tradition says that two angels (Munkar and Nakir) give a three-question pop quiz right after death to the person's spirit. "Who is your God? Who is your prophet? What is your faith?" The right answers will send you to other angels who help you pass the time until the day of resurrection and judgment. If you give the wrong answers, you'll get a head start on the punishment that you will receive at the judgment.

## Here Comes the Judge

There are some striking similarities between Islam and Christianity on the point of judgment. Both religions have these beliefs in common:

- There will be a Day of Judgment.

- It will happen at a time in the future that is known only to God.

- Everyone who has ever lived will be judged.

- Everyone is graded on a "pass or fail" basis.

- If you "pass," you go to heaven. If you "fail," then you'll spend eternity in hell.

Do you remember from high school or college that you often selected a teacher or professor based on how tough they graded? Even if you were taking a class on a "pass/fail" basis, it would be important to know the standard that the instructor used for grading. The Allah of Islam and the God of Christianity use drastically different standards for the Ultimate Judgment Day Exam.

## For Muslims: Your Good Deeds Have to Outweigh Your Bad Ones

According to the Qur'an, all human activities have been written down in books (Surah 84:6-8). Allah will judge the deeds of each person on a scale of absolute justice. The scale is used to weigh one's good deeds against his or her evil deeds. The tip of the scales will determine your fate.

> *There is one loophole that would allow a Muslim—and only a Muslim—to avoid judgment. Those who die as martyrs in defense of the Islamic faith or in a "holy war" (jihad) go directly to heaven and avoid the uncertain outcome of the judgment.*

> *Those whose balance [of good deeds] is heavy—they will attain salvation: but*

> *those whose balance is light, will be those*
> *who have lost their souls; in hell will they*
> *abide* (Surah 23:102-103).

## For Christians: You Only Need to Have Believed in Jesus

In Matthew 25, Jesus described God's grading system like this:

- ✓ He will be sitting on a throne in all his glory with his angels around him.

- ✓ All the people of all nations will be gathered in his presence.

- ✓ Like a shepherd, he will separate the "sheep" from the "goats."

- ✓ The "sheep"—all the people who accepted Jesus as their Savior during their lifetime—will go to his right side.

- ✓ The "goats"—all those who rejected a belief in Jesus—will go to his left side.

- ✓ The "sheep" will be welcomed into the kingdom of God. The "goats" will be sent to eternal punishment with Satan and the demons.

It is as simple as that. No scales. No weighing your good deeds against your bad deeds. It is just a matter of whether you put your faith in Jesus during your life.

## Heaven Is High and Hell Is Low

We'll close this chapter with what is probably a familiar subject for you: heaven and hell. We're sure that you haven't experienced either of them yet, but you've no doubt heard sermons or seen movies about them. The sermons are probably a little closer to reality than the movies, but the concepts are fairly well understood. In fact, Islam and Christianity are closely aligned on this subject.

### Heaven Is a Wonderful Place

Christians call it "heaven." Muslims often refer to it as "paradise." They are referring to the same thing (so we'll keep calling it heaven for the sake of simplicity).

For both the Muslim and the Christian, the best part about heaven is the fact that God is there. This means that those in heaven will be in the presence of God. It doesn't get any better than that. But there is more:

- Heaven is a real place.
- It is a place of unimaginable beauty.
- There is no suffering or sorrow there.
- You won't be bored in heaven.

The Qur'an says this about heaven:

> *The faithful will enjoy gentle speech,*
> *pleasant shade, and every available fruit,*
> *as well as all the cool drink and meat they*
> *desire. They will drink from a shining*
> *stream of delicious wine, from which they*
> *will suffer no intoxicating aftereffects*
> (Surah 37:45-47).

Most Christians wouldn't argue with this description (although our Southern Baptist friends might prefer to substitute coffee for the wine).

> *In the Muslim view of heaven, men are promised the companionship of young and beautiful women. We don't think the Christian view has this gender preference.*

## The "Other" Place

On the subject of hell, it doesn't make any difference whether you subscribe to the Islamic or Christian viewpoint. In either faith, you'll want to avoid hell at all costs.

Here are some of the phrases that are used in the Bible to describe hell:

- outer darkness
- furnace
- weeping and gnashing of teeth
- eternal fire
- eternal and terrible punishment
- everlasting destruction
- a lake that burns with fire and sulfur

The descriptions aren't any less graphic in the Qur'an:

- a place of unimaginable suffering
- boiling water that melts one's skin
- the taste of torment

The Muslim and the Christian both agree that hell is a real place, and the worst part about it is that you'll be separated from Allah/God for eternity.

---

## *What's That Again?*

1. For Muslims, like Christians, death is inevitable. But it isn't the end. Your soul is eternal.

2. Muslims believe that all people who have died will be resurrected at a future date for the great judgment. A widely held view in Christianity has a resurrection for Christians at the time of the rapture. While the

bodies of non-Christians may not be resurrected from the dead, their spirits will be present at the Day of Judgment.

3. In Islam and Christianity, there will be a Day of Judgment for all people. God will judge on a "pass/fail" basis.

4. Muslims believe that Allah's grading system at the judgment will involve a scale that weighs your good deeds against the bad things you have done in your life. You never know during your lifetime if you have done enough to ensure that the scale tips in favor of your good works.

5. Christians don't have to worry about a scale. The only standard by which God judges is whether a person believed in Jesus as their Savior. A belief in Jesus means that you can be assured of your eternal salvation.

6. Heaven: Be there. Hell: Don't wanna go there.

## Dig Deeper

There is an excellent chapter on Islam in *The World's Religions: Understand the Living Faiths*, edited by Dr. Peter B. Clarke. It is published by Reader's Digest, but don't look for one of those pint-sized, condensed books. This is a coffee-table book.

We think you will find that *Bruce & Stan's*® *Guide to Bible Prophecy* will give you a good overview of "end of the world" events like the rapture and judgment. There's also a good chapter on heaven. We learned a lot from this book.

We relied heavily on another excellent source of information about the Muslim faith. Check out *Islam: An Introduction for Christians*, edited by Paul Varo Martinson. This book has an objective analysis of the Islamic faith.

## Moving On

Our overview of the Muslim faith is now complete, but you'll notice that there is one remaining chapter in the book. We've got a little bit more to say, but it isn't so much about the tenets of Islam. We have devoted the last chapter to giving you a challenge. Now that you are a semi-expert on what Muslims believe, we think you ought to do something with that knowledge.

# Chapter 7

## Sharing Your Faith: God's Good News Is for Everyone

> *Go into all the world and preach the Good News to everyone, everywhere.*
>
> —Jesus Christ

Congratulations! If you've actually read this entire Pocket Guide to this point (in other words, you haven't skipped ahead to read the last chapter like we sometimes do), then you are among a select group of people. Just by learning the basics of Islam, you have done what few Westerners have ever done.

A lot of people claim to understand Islam— they think those street demonstrators in the West Bank or Islamabad as reported on CNN represent all Muslims—but few really do. You, on the other hand, at least have a basic knowledge of what a Muslim believes.

So what do you do with what you know? Do you file it under the category of "That's nice," or do you put your knowledge into practice? Obviously, you have an interest in Islam, or you wouldn't have read this book. And now that you've read it, you want to do something. Well, that's what this final chapter is all about. We want to help you do something with what you know, and not just because it makes us feel good, but because it's what Jesus wants you to do.

*Bruce & Stan*

# Chapter 7

# Sharing Your Faith: God's Good News Is for Everyone

*What's Ahead*

➤ Share the Good News
➤ The Fields Are Ripe for Harvest
➤ The Tide Is Turning
➤ How Do We Reach Them?

We've done our best to give you the truth about the Christian faith and about the beliefs of Muslims, but we have left one important thing out. As a Christian, it's not enough to know the truth about God and the truth about Islam. That's where you *begin,* but you can't stop there. There's something else you have to do.

## Share the Good News

There's more to your faith than knowing
what you believe. Now you need to share
the Good News of your relationship with
Jesus. And this isn't just us talking. Jesus
personally gave the command to share the
Good News about himself—that he is the
only way to have a personal relationship
with God forever.

Jesus came to earth to save sinners, to turn
them from darkness to light (John 1:4-5).
But he never intended this salvation to be a
private matter. There was never an option
for people saved by the death and resurrection of Jesus to hide their light under a
basket. God sent Jesus into the world to
provide salvation, and now Jesus is
sending you into the world to share the
Good News about your salvation—to
everyone, everywhere.

## The Fields Are Ripe for Harvest

Jesus set the example for us while he was
on earth. The Bible says: "Jesus traveled
through all the cities and villages of that
area, teaching in the synagogues and
announcing the Good News about the

Kingdom" (Matthew 9:35). And wherever he went, he felt great compassion for those who were lost, "because their problems were so great and they didn't know where to go for help" (Matthew 9:36). Jesus told his followers:

> *The harvest is so great, but the workers are so few. So pray to the Lord who is in charge of the harvest; ask him to send out more workers for his fields* (Matthew 9:37-38).

The *field* is anyplace in the world where the Good News needs to be heard, the *workers* are Christians who need to share the Good News, and the *harvest* is that time when lost people give their hearts to Jesus.

And where do you suppose is the greatest potential for harvest? If you're going by sheer numbers, the Muslim world wins hands down. With more than 1 billion followers who have put their faith in Allah by believing the message of Muhammad as told in the Qur'an, there is no greater mission field. By the same token, there is no place where the workers are so few.

> *Approximately 80 percent of Muslims have never heard the Good News, making Muslims the least evangelized people in the world.*

## The Tide Is Turning

The world of Islam once seemed so mysterious and distant, but that is changing. As Muslims have fanned out into non-Arab countries, Christians are beginning to see an unprecedented opportunity to share the gospel (that's another word for "Good News"). In his book *Planting Churches in Muslim Cities* Dr. Greg Livingstone asks: "Could God have actually engineered these Muslims to our countries to learn of Christ and his forgiveness?"

As Muslims migrate to countries like the United States (estimates range between 2 and 7 million Muslims are living in the U.S.), they are becoming more and more aware of "religious Christians" (this is in contrast to the belief held in Muslim-dominated countries that American Christians and infidels are one and the same). Serious Muslims are beginning to see that they have a lot in common with Christians who are serious about their faith.

## How Do We Reach Them?

If you are serious about reaching your Muslim neighbor, friend, or coworker with the Good News of Jesus, then there are some simple yet effective things you can do.

### Obey Jesus' Command

We've already talked about this. If we are to call ourselves true followers of Jesus, we need to obey his command to share the Good News with everyone, everywhere. *Everyone* means everyone you know—your family, your friends, your coworkers, people God puts in your path. *Everywhere* means wherever you go.

### Pray

Pray and ask God to make you aware of the people he puts in your path. Ask for wisdom when you talk to people about the Lord. And when you don't know what to pray for, realize that the Holy Spirit will pray on your behalf (Romans 8:26-27).

### Look for Opportunities

You can be sure that God will send people your way. You just have to keep your eyes open and be ready to respond. We know a Christian woman who works with a number of Muslims. After September 11, she noticed one of her coworkers, a Muslim woman, was especially self-conscious. So our friend told the woman that she didn't blame her for the attacks. Little did she realize how comforting those simple words were for the Muslim woman, who brought a plate full of cookies for her new friend the next day. It may not seem like much, but God doesn't need much to change a heart.

### Find Common Ground

In the preceding chapters, we've pointed out the differences between Christianity and Islam, and we've also highlighted the similarities. Use these to find some common ground with the Muslims you meet. Talk about God and his sovereignty, about sin and the need for salvation. Emphasize God's love and mercy.

### Talk About the Qur'an and the Bible

Remember how much Muslims revere the Qur'an. Express admiration for this loyalty, and talk about how you see the Bible as the message of God to all people. Point out the similarities between the two holy books, and gently show how the Bible is the most reliable holy book of all.

### Lift Up Jesus

This is an area that will separate Christians from Muslims more than any other, but you can't back off. Help Muslims understand that Christianity is not just a religion, but a personal relationship with Jesus Christ (1 John 1:3). Muslims will tell you that the designation of Jesus as the Son of God contradicts the oneness of God. Respond by saying that Jesus isn't another God, but is one with God the Father, just as the Holy Spirit is one with God the Father. It is not three gods, but one God in three Persons.

### Love Your Neighbor

If you know some Muslims, love them. As Muslims see the love of Christ lived through your life, they will be compelled by the Person of Christ in your life.

## What's That Again?

1. Jesus commands that we share the Good News with everyone, everywhere.

2. There is no greater mission field than the Muslim world.

3. There are some practical things you can do to reach Muslims: Obey what Jesus said, pray, look for opportunities, find common ground, talk about the Qur'an and the Bible, lift up Jesus, and love them.

## Dig Deeper

*Planting Churches in Muslim Cities* by Greg Livingstone has practical applications for anyone wanting to reach Muslims, even if your mission field is the office.

William Saal's *Reaching Muslims for Christ* breaks the myth that Muslims are unreachable.

The final book we want to recommend is (what else) *Bruce & Stan's® Pocket Guide to Sharing Your Faith.* Hey, what can we say? It's a good little book.

## Moving On

The apostle Paul was the greatest missionary ever. In the first century Paul carried the Good News about Jesus to the far ends of the known world. Once Paul was in Athens, and he couldn't help but notice idols everywhere in the city. One idol in particular had an inscription that read: *To an Unknown God.* As Paul witnessed to the Greek philosophers, who were asking him about his faith, Paul said this about the Unknown God:

*You have been worshiping him without knowing who he is, and now I wish to tell you about him. He is the God who made the world and everything in it. Since he is Lord of heaven and earth, he doesn't live in manmade temples, and human hands can't serve his needs—for he has no needs. He himself gives life and breath to everything, and he satisfies every need there is....His purpose in all of this was that the nations should seek after God and perhaps feel their way toward him and find him—though he is not far from any one of us* (Acts 17:23-25,27).

That's the message we need to bring to the Muslim people today, wherever they are. The God they seek is not far from them. He may be far from their culture, but God is not far from their hearts. May this be an encouragement and a challenge to you as you share the Good News about God and his plan to save us through Jesus Christ.

## About the Authors

Bruce Bickel is a lawyer, but he didn't start out that bad. After college, he considered the noble profession of a stand-up comic, but he had to abandon that dream because he is not very funny. As a lawyer, he makes people laugh (but it is not on purpose).

Stan Jantz is a marketing consultant. From the time he was a little kid, Stan's family owned a chain of Christian bookstores, so he feels very comfortable behind the counter.

Bruce and Stan spend their free time as "cultural observers" (they made that term up). They watch how God applies to real life. Together they have written more than 30 books.

## Other Books by the Guys

Bruce & Stan's® Guide to God

Bruce & Stan's® Guide to the Bible

Bruce & Stan's® Guide to How It All Began

Bruce & Stan's® Guide to Bible Prophesy

Bruce & Stan's® Pocket Guide to Prayer

Bruce & Stan's® Pocket Guide to Sharing Your Faith

Bruce & Stan's® Pocket Guide to Studying Your Bible

Bruce & Stan's® Pocket Guide to Knowing Jesus

Bruce & Stan's® Pocket Guide to Islam

Bruce & Stan's® Search for the Meaning of Life

God Is in the Small Stuff (and It All Matters)

Real Life Has No Expiration Date

Real Life to the Extreme

Simple Matters

Bruce and Stan would enjoy hearing from you. (If you've got something nice to say, then don't hold back. If you have a criticism, then be gentle.) The best way to contact them is:

E-mail: **guide@bruceandstan.com**

Snail Mail: Bruce & Stan
P.O. Box 25565
Fresno, CA 93729-5565

You can learn more than you ever wanted to know about Bruce and Stan by visiting their Web site: **www.bruceandstan.com**